TOM GOURDIE was awarded the M.B.E. for his services to calligraphy, and has been engaged for many years in the study of handwriting. His methods have recently been adopted by the Swedish Board of Education for experimental use in Swedish schools, and he has lectured to students at Colleges of Education in this country and on the Continent.

INDEX

The Ladybird book of
HANDWRITING

by TOM GOURDIE, M.B.E.

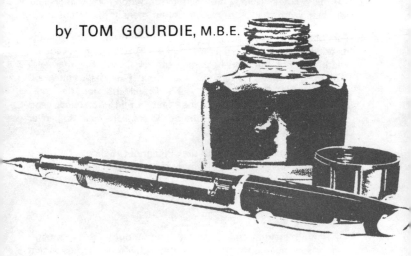

Publishers Wills & Hepworth Ltd   Loughborough

First published 1968   ©   *Printed in England*

This writing book is intended for young children just learning to write and also for all those who, not so young, wish to improve their handwriting, having scribbled long enough.

The following notes will assist parents and teachers using this book.

Recommended working tools

1. The Black Prince or any similar pencil which is thick enough to afford an easy hold for children.

2. The Esterbrook Water Colour pencils which have a felt tip and therefore encourage a loose hold, since they make a mark so easily.

3. The Esterbrook Gem Fine Writer for writing on paper and for finer work than the Water Colour pencil just mentioned.

4. For pen and ink, the Platignum fountain pens are recommended, using the standard series 'Broad' and 'Medium' width nibs for the non-italic part of the book. For the italic section the Broad, Medium and then Fine italic nibs are recommended, beginning with the Broad nib for the preliminary exercises and for the first writing practice, and then where the writing is obviously smaller, changing over to a Medium width.

5. For general classroom use, the Platignum School Cartridge pen is the obvious choice, since it eliminates the use of an ink-well and at the same time gives one the advantage of the splendid range of nibs provided by this firm.

NOTE

All writing instruments must be long enough, thick enough and responsive enough to enable children to use them easily and without tension. The ball point pen is therefore most emphatically discouraged.

Holding the pencil

It is important that the pencil should be held in the natural way — by the thumb and forefinger and supported just before the first joint of the middle finger. The forefinger should rest on the pencil about $1\frac{1}{2}$" from the pencil point and the pencil should therefore point into the paper at an angle of 45° and also be held pointed to the writing line at the same angle.

The hand should rest on the paper supported by the side, the fingers slightly crooked but not turned in towards the palm of the hand. The pencil must be long enough at all times so that it lies cradled between the thumb and forefinger. Pencil stumps and short pieces of chalk must not be used.

Angle of pen to paper

Angle of pen to line

The writer should be seated comfortably, feet flat on the floor and the desk sloping slightly and high enough to support the elbow comfortably. The paper should be tilted down to the left – and for the left-handed to the right.

The left-handed should be encouraged to hold the pencil pointed towards the body – almost parallel to the angle used by the right-handed. To enable the left-handed to acquire the thick and thin strokes of italic, the Platignum left-oblique nib is recommended, which thus dispenses with the need to twist the wrist which would otherwise be necessary.

Movement in handwriting

The natural movement of the hand, pivoting from the wrist, is essential to good, fluent handwriting so the preliminary exercises are devised for this purpose. The fingers must never move the pencil or pen but serve simply to hold it while the whole hand does the actual work. This ensures that back-hand will be eliminated, for it is the flexing of the fingers (thumb and forefinger) that produces this unfortunate effect.

Paper

Blank paper is suggested for the preliminary exercises and for most of the first part of the book. Where lined paper is used, let the lines be wide enough apart (say ½″) so that they serve to guide and not restrain the writing.

Preliminary exercises towards gaining control over the writing instrument and in co-ordinating hand and eye. Horizontal, vertical and diagonal directions.

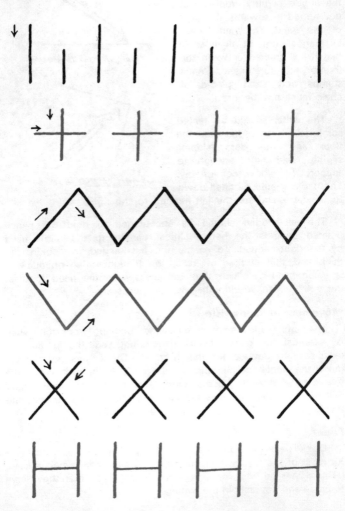

Circular movements in clockwise and anti-clockwise directions.

The two principal movements of handwriting.

Pages 9-12 introduce the alphabet in its simplest form. First the 'clockwise' letters.

m n m n

h n h n h

k n k n k

h k h k h

b n b n b

p n p n p

More 'clockwise' letters.

r r r r r r r r

r r r r r r r

h k h k h k h

b p b p b p b

n m r m n r

b h k p h k b

The 'anti-clockwise' letters, grouped in families.

u i u i u i u i u i

r l r l r l r l r l

y u y u y u y u

a u a u a u a u

d g d g d g d g d

q u q u q u q u q

More 'anti-clockwise' letters. (The final line is an exercise in turning the letters upside down).

oceoceoceoce

fjfjfjfjfj

sosososos

vwvwv

xzxzxz

bqhynu

The letters grouped according to their basic movements.

mm mm

mnhkbpr

uu uuu

itluy, adgq,

oec, vw, fj,

sxz

The letters in alphabetic order. (Sandwiching letters with 'm' is an ideal way to acquire fluency of movement).

abcdefgh

ijklmno

pqrstuv

wxyz

amamamama

The capital letters, beginning with those letters comprising vertical, horizontal and diagonal strokes.

ITITITIT

LELFLEL

HIHIHI

AVAVA

WYWWY

XKZXKZ

The capital letters showing the round letters and the two widest letters, M and W.

DGDGDG

BPBRBPBR

OQCOQC

MWMWM

NUNUNU

SJSJSJS

Showing both alphabets. Note relative heights of capital and ascender letters, the latter being slightly taller. The small letter alphabet is compressed, in contrast to the round and open character of the capital alphabet, O in the former being oval whilst round in the latter.

Ascender ⟶

a A b B c C

d D e E f F g G

⟵ *Descender*

h H i I j J k K

l L m M n N

o O p P q Q r R

s S t T u U v V

Christian names used as a first exercise in bringing both alphabets together.

wW xX yY

and zZ

Adam·Brian

Charles

David·Ella

Frank

George·Hugh

Ian

James·Kate

Lilias

Marion·Neil

Olga

Peter·Queen

Rachel

Susan·Tom

Ursula

Vera·Wilma

X·Y·Z

In order to provide cursiveness, the small letters are given additional 'entry' and 'exit' strokes wherever necessary.

ɔɔɔ · ιιι · ɔɔɔ

n m r m n

i i i · u u · t t t

l h k l h k l h

a d · j p · a d

v w x y z

The alphabet in its complete form, with the clockwise letters in red.

a b c d e f g h

i j k l m n o p

q r s s t t t u v

w x y α z or ʒ

nun · run

mummy

Joining up the letters. The groups in red join naturally to the groups in black and also to the ascender group, using diagonal joining strokes.

a c d e h i k l m

n u z

e f i j m n o p r s

t u v w x y z

ae af ai aj am an

ao ap ar as at au

av aw ax ay a a z

ab ah ak al

Some letters join from the top so that horizontal joining strokes normally result from them. When followed by ascender letters, the horizontal joining stroke naturally becomes a diagonal. When this group is followed by 'e' no join is made except from 'f'.

The pen is lifted before a, c, d, g and q - but make sure that it is lifted at the top of the diagonal upstroke to ensure enough spacing.

The pen is lifted after g, j, q, y and z, but it is suggested that a join may follow z in order to form this letter more easily.

fortvw

oa ob oc od of og oh oi

oj ok ol om on oo op oq

or oz ot ou ov ow ox oy oz

e: fe, oe, re, te, ve, we

aa: aa, ac, ad, ag, aq.

go, jo, quo, yo, zo, zo.

The alphabet with joining strokes. Although it is suggested that pen-lifts should follow b, p and s, it is desirable in the case of those letters to join from the second one in order to avoid consecutive pen-lifts. Good rhythm depends on this.

abcdefg

hijklmnopqu

rsstttuvwxyz

abba, appa

assa

bay, gay, jay, pay,

quay, say, axis, ye,

zee.

Some double letters.

Double 't' is like an enlarged 'u' with one stroke carried through both uprights.

Use the alternative 's' (as shown) after a diagonal join and use the complete 's' at the beginning of a word—or when 's' is preceded by a pen-lift.

tt : *butter, fitter, potter, sitter.*

ll : *ball, call, doll, hill, mill, tell.*

ff : *off, offer, suffer.*

ss : *misses, hiss, passes, tosses.*

The list of Christian names written with joining strokes between the letters.

Adam Brian
Charles David
Ella Frank
George Hugh
Ian James Kate
Lilias Marion
Neil Olga Peter
Queen Rachel

Susan Tom
Ursula Vera
Wilma XYZ
My Christian
name is my first
name and my
Surname is my
family name.

The following pages 29-33 give writing practice combined with vocabulary enlargement.

A is for apple, air,
    axe, angel.
B is for boy, bird,
    book, blue.
C is for cook, cat,
    car, coat.
D is for dog, day,
    dust, door.
E is for ear, egg,
    exit, eye.
F is for fire, food,
    fairy, fly.

G is for good, goat,
girl, grass.
H is for hand, hair,
home, heel.
I is for ink, ill,
ice, iron.
J is for jam, jump,
joy, jet.
K is for king, keep,
knee, kilt.
L is for lock, lamb,
lump, log.

M is for mother,
man, moon.
N is for net, near,
nose, noon.
O is for old, open,
over, oak.
P is for pie, play,
poor, paper.
Q is for queen,
quick, quill.
R is for rose, red,
rope, ride.

S is for sunny,
sweet, shell.

T is for tea, toe,
trip, tail.

U is for uncle,
under, ugly.

V is for van, verse,
vest, voice.

W is for way, well,
wish, wing.

X is for Xmas, x-ray.

On this page is an exercise of considerable importance —
the sandwiching of 'n' between pairs of identical letters.
Pen-lifts are shown by a red dot.

Y is for you, yellow,
    yard, year.
Z is for zoo, zip,
    zebra, zoom.
ana, bnb, cnc, dnd,
ene, fnf, gng, hnh,
ini, jnj, knk, lnl,
mnm, nmn, pnp,
qnq, rnr, sns, tnt,
unu, vnv, wnw,
xnx, yny & znz.

Pages 34-41 give further writing practice. Writing must inevitably be used as a means to an end, so even at this stage the learner must be encouraged to regard hand-writing in this way and therefore to try to add to the lists that have been given as practice material in this book.

Clothes.

Hat and coat.

Boots and shoes.

Vest and pants.

Shoes and socks.

Collar and tie.

Skirt and jumper.

Jacket and trousers.

Scarf and gloves.

Shirt and blouse:

Stockings and
 garters.

Common things.
Table and chairs.
Tea and sugar.
Cup and saucer.
Knife and fork.
Horse and cart.
Bacon and egg.
Fish and chips.
Salt and pepper.
Needle and thread.
Spade and pail.
Brush and comb.

Making sound.
Banging the drum.
Blowing the
   trumpet.
Singing a song.
Whistling a
   tune.
Clapping hands.
Stamping feet.
Ringing bells.
Clashing the
   cymbals.

Noises.

The cock is crowing.

The dog is barking.

The geese are cackling.

The pigs are grunting.

The sheep are bleating.

The cows are lowing.

The owl is screeching.

The door is squeaking.

The birds are singing.

The lion is roaring.

The baby is crying.

The Months.
Thirty days hath
September,
April, June and
November.
All the rest have
thirty-one,
Except February alone
which has twenty-
eight days clear
And twenty-nine
in each Leap year.

January, February,
March, April, May,
June, July, August,
September, October,
November and
December – *the year.*

Monday, Tuesday,
Wednesday,
Thursday, Friday,
Saturday and
Sunday – *the week.*

One, two, buckle
my shoe.
Three, four, open
the door.
Five, six, pick up
sticks.
Seven, eight, lay
them straight,
Nine, ten, a big
fat hen
Laid an egg for
gentlemen.

One, two, three, four,
  five,
Once I caught a
  fish alive,

Six, seven, eight,
  nine, ten,
Then I let it go
  again.

Why did you let it go?
Because it bit my
  finger so!

Strictly speaking, we have so far been doing italic writing, but until now the pencil or pointed pen has been used providing us with a cord line, which is all the same thickness unless variation of pressure is made. To achieve the natural contrast of stroke which most people associate with italic writing, the chisel-edged pen must be used, and this requires special practice. The pen must be held pointed into the paper and to the line, at 45°, and to ensure that this is achieved these exercises have been devised. Use a broad nib.

The special italic two-stroke 'e' is recommended. The simple 'e' must still be used, but only where 'e' begins a word or where it follows a pen-lift: at all other times use the two-stroke version. The two-stroke 'e' is made first almost like a 'c', to which a loop is added and from the loop the joining stroke connects to the next letter. This page shows the complete italic alphabet written with the italic pen, using a broad nib.

ccccccccc

eeeeeeeeeee

abcdefgh

ijklmnop

qrstuvwx

yaz

The alphabet, joined wherever possible. Note once again the relative heights of capital and ascender letters.

abcdefghij

klmnopq

rsstuvwx

yαz

AaBbCcD

dEeFf

Continuing with the broad nib, it is suggested that the learner copies this and the following page.

Adam Brian

Charles David

Ella Frank

George Hugh

Ian James Kate

Lilias Marion

Neil Olga Peter

Queen Rachel

Susan Thomas

Ursula Vera
William XYZ

ambmcmdmem
fngmhmimjmk
mlmnmompm
qumrmsmtmu
mvmwmxmy
mzm
ama·bmb·cmc·

Pages 47-51 suggest further writing practice using a medium italic nib and finally, if it is desired, try the fine italic nib.

One, two buckle
  my shoe.
Three, four open
  the door.
Five, six, pick up
  sticks.
Seven, eight, lay
  them straight.
Nine, ten, a big
  fat hen
Laid an egg for
  gentlemen.

One, two, three, four,
five,
Once I caught a fish
alive,

Six, seven, eight, nine
ten,
Then I let it go
again.

Why did you let it go?
Because it bit my
finger so!

The Time.
There are sixty seconds
in one minute,
sixty minutes in
one hour,
twenty-four hours
in one day,
and three hundred
and sixty-five days
in the year. A Leap
year has one more
day.

The Lark makes its nest
in a hollow in the ground,
often in a hoof-mark, and
just lines the hollow with
a little grass. It is a very
difficult nest to find, being
so small.

Robins often build their
nests in garden sheds, but
they also build them in old
boots, tin cans and so on.

One of our most attractive insects is the Ladybird, with its bright red back spotted with black. Those pretty little beetles are welcomed by wise gardeners, for their larvae destroy the green-flies that attack roses and many other plants. Lady-birds are, indeed, as useful as they are attractive.

Variations showing the more formal italic hand—a style suitable for writing out verse, wedding invitations, etc.

Pen exercises.

un un un un un un

mw mw mw mw m

vr vr vr vr vr vr vr vr

bg bg bg bg bg bg bg bg

hy hy hy hy hy hy h

dq dq dq dq dq dq d

ch ch ch ch ch ch ch

wh wh wh wh wh w

abba abba abba ab

opdo opdo opdo opdo op

cl cl cl cl cl cl cl cl cl